They call me a Rag Picker

by Delaney Lott Harmond

They call me a Rag Picker

Library of Congress No. 99-95264
Harmond (Lott), Delaney
They call me a Rag Picker
ISBN 0-9670435-0-6
Cover Design & layout by Scott A. Markham
Editing by Kathleen S. Markham

First printing July 1999
10 9 8 7 6 5 4 3 2 1

Publisher: Designs by Delaney
SAN 299-9099
4221 68th Street Ct. NW, Gig Harbor, WA 98335

Printed in the United States of America

Table of Contents

"I dedicate this book to my beloved husband, Bill Harmond. Without him by my side and without his Christ-like patience, caring love and all that he is, there would be no Rag Picker stories."

——— *DLH*

Acknowledgements

'Thank you' to all those who helped me put this book together.

Without my friend, Janet Robertson, this would still be sitting on my heart and in my mind only. Janet spent hours typing, sorting and encouraging me. At first, we prayed together, cried and laughed over this project. Janet was often living out these stories right beside me in Jamaica, on the streets and in our home. God gave me a very special friend.

I also want to thank my wonderful father-in-law, Jesse Harmond. He encouraged me both vocally and financially. Thanks, Dad!

I also owe a big thank you to my Mom and Daddy, Grover and Annie Mae Lott. Even though things were not always easy at home, they always made sure I took my sisters Patsy, Linda, Billie Sue and little brother Derry Lee to the Baptist Church and Sunday School. There, I accepted Jesus at the age of 13. Thanks, Mom and Daddy!

Blessings also to Scott and Kathy Markham for all their expert help with editing, wonderful graphics and giving birth to my book.

There are so many more to thank, but, most of all I thank God for letting me tell of his *wonderfulness!*

——— *Delaney Lott Harmond*
April 1999

Foreword

"Delaney will always be remembered as one of the most colorful characters I've ever known. For over four years I've observed firsthand Delaney's love for the unlovely, the poor, the castoffs and rejects. I've watched in amazement as she has poured her love and life into these hopeless cases. I've seen them changed and transformed through this wonderful instrument of God's love. Calcutta had its Mother Theresa. Gig Harbor has Delaney."

———— *Pastor David Ravenhill*
(Author of "For God's Sake Grow Up")

Ron Post (N.W. Founder), Bill Harmond, Rod Andrews

"In the game of life, Delaney Harmond is an All-Star. Her unselfish nature is refreshing in a culture that often values getting over giving. If the takers eat better, but the givers sleep better, insomnia should never be a problem for Delaney. From the streets of Tacoma, Washington, to the dump communities of Mexico, her heart reaches out to the less fortunate and those who are struggling with their lives. Teen-aged kids whom the system has rejected, have a special place in Delaney's life. Her love for these troubled teens is tough, yet unconditional.

Life in Delaney's world is always an adventure. Political correctness never seems to be a priority and forgiveness is often easier for her to seek than permission. God blessed her with an overwhelming capacity to love the unlovable. She also has the ability to turn an ordinary plane ride with a mission team to Mexico, into a most memorable happening for all those on board. Because she lives life on the edge, she'll never be accused of taking up too much room on the planet.

This world is a better place because of the value Delaney's unbridled zest for life has added. Her unashamedly Christian witness shines brightest when she bathes the children of the Mexico City dumps, where she traveled repeatedly with Northwest Medical Teams. We are blessed to have the privilege of working with her to touch the neediest of our world. Her boundless energy and her servant heart are an inspiration to all of us who are fortunate to know her."

——— *Dick Fredericks*
Director of Seattle N.W. Medical Team

*Daughter inlaw Stephanie (Billups), Dan, Delaney, and
Bill Harmond*

I'm so proud to be the
mother of sons Dan and Wayne
Harmond. I thank God for
them and my daughter inlaw
Stephanie. We're looking forward to receiving our latest
addition to the family, grand-
son Matthew.

Wayne Harmond

Stephanie and Dan Harmond

They call me a Rag Picker

What is a rag picker? Is that a bag lady as I first thought? *No!* A rag picker is a person who spends most of her time rescuing humans from life's refuse pile. There she sees the throwaways, the unlovable, unwanted and the lost.

The rag picker stops, listens and starts pulling the rags of humanity from the pile. They clean up, love, pray for and sometimes take the rags home.

I've heard that during the war and the depression days, people gathered real rags from the streets and garbage piles. They washed, cleaned and sorted them out to make beautiful rag rugs and many useful things.

As the women in our Chapel Hill Bible Study explained why they called me a rag picker, I began to cry.

——— *Delaney Lott Harmond*

1
The Slasher

There was a feeling of joy and excitement that beautiful day in August. Bill and I were headed for my high school reunion. Wow! My 40th year reunion. Each year that we attend I can't help but wonder, "Where are my young classmates and what are all these old people doing here?" Then I pass a mirror and I remember, "Oh! Yes! Those were years gone by, but I still feel 16 in my heart." And, yes, that feeling still gets me into trouble.

Our party was to start at 6 p.m. at the Albany Country Club. Bill and his father were going golfing together that morning. So, I had time to spend with my sister, Patt Derrah. We met in the huge parking lot near the K Mart shopping center. Patt and I discussed whose car to drive to see my old classmate and long time buddy, Ron Dittmer. Patt finally talked me into leaving my car. We knew it would be safe as many people were coming and going, and about 100 other cars were all around mine.

We had a great time with Ron and were eagerly waiting for the evening when we would be with more great friends at the reunion. After two or three hours Patt and I bid Ron good bye and headed back to the parking lot. As we drove toward my car, we saw several people around it, including two policemen. My day was really getting exciting now.

The police asked if that was my New Yorker. I said, "Yes, what's wrong?"

Then I saw that my tires had been slashed and one was ripped open and flat. "Oh! Great!" I started praying silently. "God, What is the meaning of this? So many car tires to slash and why was mine chosen?"

Little did I know God was about to answer that question loud and clear. The police and witness told me that two little boys, gang members both about ten or eleven years old, had walked around the parking lot, looked over the cars and decided mine would be the car they would hack with the machete and stab with the sharp knife they had hidden in their clothes.

The policemen warned me not to go after the boys, who they felt could be dangerous. Several other policemen were chasing them and had tracked them to an underground passway near Waverly Lake. After three hours, they still couldn't find them.

The policemen took down the information on who we were, where we were from, and how long we were going to be there. I told my sister, "I'm going to have to call Les Schwaub to come here and fix my spare tire and put it on". I was in a hurry to meet Bill since it was already past 4:00. I talked her into leaving.

A couple of men came by and saw that I needed help. They had seen the boys who had done the damage. They fixed my spare, put it on for me and helped me get over to Les Schwab.

The policemen had asked me what I wanted to do about the boys. I was feeling really angry. As I was thinking about it the thought came to me, "I would like to find the boys and have them pay for the tires."

It took quite a while to repair the tires, so I rested in the back seat of the car. As I was lying there I prayed "Okay God. Now what do we do? Why did this happen? What should we do with these two little boys?" I was lying there crying, feeling devastated, and in awe that two little boys would have tire slashing in their hearts and could do this. The Lord told me so plainly, "Go find the boy that destroyed the tire. Take him home, love him, care for him and show this boy that with Jesus' love he doesn't have to do this. He doesn't have to be angry and slicing out at people or things." I thought, "Oh God! Take the kid home? Man, here we go again! Could this be our next boy?"

The car was finished, and I paid the man and left. I called Bill and told him that I'd be at the country club in an hour. I was just a few blocks from where my tires were slashed. There was a fork in the road with one way to the freeway and the other to Corvallis. At the stop sign I prayed, "Lord, if you want me to find this kid, please give me a sign". Suddenly I was startled because as I looked up to the right there was a little trailer park. It was starting to get a little dark. Suddenly the sign that said "Trailer Park" lit up with bulbs all around it going on. This took my breath away as I realized that I had asked for a sign!

I had to go find out why that sign was blinking and beckoning me. I drove my car to the office, parked the car and rushed up to the door. I banged loudly on the door. This little grandpa opened the door and said, "May I help you?"

I said, "Excuse me. Have you seen two little boys? The police described them as being about ten or eleven years old. They had on black Raider sweatshirts, hats, cutoff shorts, and black tennis shoes. One had a machete and the other had a sharper pointed knife."

He looked at me and said, "Boy, have I seen them. Right now they're here in my backyard at the end of this road where my property ends at the graveyard. One has a machete and is cutting blackberry vines. The other is over there breaking beer bottles."

I said, "Are you sure? How do you know they are there?"

He said, "I was riding my bicycle around there and ran over the broken glass from the beer bottles. Both my bicycle tires are flat."

I said, "My tires were flattened too, only in a different way."

He said, "Come with me."

I followed him down a path through a row of trailers. On the other side of the fence, were the boys. You could see where they had hacked down the blackberry vines. As I watched them, the two brats jumped over the fence and headed towards a dirty yellow house, which was badly in need of paint. There were broken down bicycles, cars, trucks, and an old trailer beside the house. A big old dog was out front and there were some men in cutoff sleeveless shirts and bluejeans. There was a big American flag draped across the window. The boys ran up to the house and slammed the door.

The Grandpa asked, "Is that them?"

I said, "Well, I'm sure it is. They fit the description and have the knives."

He said, "Well, let's go back to the office and call the police to tell them that you found them."

I said, "Thank you for taking your time."

He said, "No problem. Those two kids are always up to something around here."

We went back and called the police. I said to them, "Hey guys, guess what? You spent over three hours looking for the little boys, but I found both of them. Here's their address and their description."

The policeman asked, "How did you find them?"

I told him, "The Lord just led me right to them."

He said, "Do you want to press charges?"

I answered, "Yes, I do."

He said, "We'll come right away and arrest them. There's nothing else you can do right now. Go on to your reunion. We'll talk to you tomorrow."

So I said, "You know, I do want the boys arrested. And, I do want their parents to know what they did. I want them to be responsible. But, when we go home tomorrow, I would also like to take the boy that did all the damage home with us."

The policeman said, "You what?"

I said, "You heard me right. I want to take the boy

home with me."

I could see him thinking, "Do you do this often?"

I said, "If the Lord gives me a kid, I take him. We've had 20-30 boys already that were hurt and needed love. I don't know anything about this kid. In my heart and with God telling me, I know that I'm supposed to take that boy home with me. I'm sure that he will go back to Gig Harbor with me."

The policeman said to me, "Delaney, the only thing that kid needs is a lethal shot."

I pondered that in my heart and thought, "What a terrible thing for a policeman and a father to say."

I asked him why he said that. He said, "Well, you know I have teenagers, and I've got a kid that's a little uncontrollable, too. But, not as bad as this one." He indicated that he meant what he said.

I thought, "Oh God, just protect the kid! I do want to bring him home with me."

The policeman said, "In the first place, there will be a court hearing before a judge. The father will not show up for the boy. We know who the kid is. His name is Trav, and his father is a single parent. He's always in trouble and runs wild. He does have a probation officer that is surely not going to give him to you. And we are not going to recommend that you take him. And another thing, the judge will never let you take an eleven-year old boy 300 miles from Albany, Oregon to Gig Harbor, Washington. I can't believe you are even thinking about it. I'm sure it will never happen. But, I'm writing down the report and will put in your request. We'll just see what happens."

So, I said, "Okay. That's done" and I jumped back
in the car and hurried to meet my husband at the country
club to tell him about my adventures. I told my cool and
collected Bill what happened. He just shook his head and
said, "Another adventure!" I told Bill that I asked to take
the kid home with us, and he said, "Well, if that's God's
will then we will get the boy."

The next morning I called the police to see what was
happening. The boys were arrested and taken to the jail.
They talked to them and threatened to keep them over
night. They were sent home in custody of their fathers.
The hearing was set for the next Thursday, so we couldn't
take them home with us this time, but we headed back to
Gig Harbor praying about it.

I stayed home all day Thursday, anxiously waiting
and praying. Early in the afternoon the phone rang. It
was the parole officer. She gave me her name and said
she was at the courthouse. They had just had the hearing.
Trav, his father, and the policeman were all there. She
said, "I can't believe this. This is the most unique hearing we have ever had. We can't believe you would want
to take Trav home. Mrs. Harmond, another thing that we
find hard to believe is that the judge said he will put the
boy in your custody for a couple of weeks. With the
father's permission, you can come and get him." The
judge, the policeman, the parole officer and the father had
all agreed this would be a turning point in the boy's life if
I would be willing to take the boy back to Gig Harbor.

I started to squeal, and then l was laughing and crying at the same time. I said, "I knew I would get him!
I'll be there this weekend to pick him up!"

Then she said, "Delaney, the father would like to talk to you. Trav is also right here and would like to talk to you."

I said, "sure!" and talked to the father first. He spoke in a very low and mild voice. He said he was very sorry that his son had done this. He didn't understand either, but if I did want to bring him home, he would turn custody over to us for a couple of weeks.

Then I talked to Trav. He was quiet and shy and didn't have too much to say. He couldn't understand why I wanted to bring him home with me.

I told him that I did want him to be responsible and there were consequences for what he did. He would have to pay for the tire, even if he had to work for it. I said, "Okay Trav. We'll be there to get you this next weekend."

About that time our son Wayne was visiting from Hawaii. I hollered to him, "Wayne! I did get Trav!" He said, "I knew it, I knew it!" We grabbed each other, and Wayne nicknamed him "the little slasher."

That weekend we headed back to Albany taking our Eagle Scout friend, Ron Lambert, with us. Ron could hardly wait to meet this Trav.

We struggled finding the house through the run down neighborhood. We felt sad as we came upon the beat up cars, garbage and old rags in the saddest parts of Albany. Even in all the years I lived there, I had never been down in that section.

When we found the house, we went to the door and Trav's father, Tim, met us. He was kind to us and invited us in. He called to Trav who was out back with a couple of baby goats. We went out the back door where I saw a healthy looking, stout eleven-year-old boy standing under the apple tree feeding apples to the goats.

I said, "Hi Trav. I'm Delaney."

He had his head down, but slowly looked up and said, "Hi Delaney."

I walked over to him and put my arm around him and said, "Are you packed and ready to go home with us?"

He said, "Yeah, I'm ready to go."

I told him, "I'm sure we have lots of things to talk about. We need to get to know each other. We've got to trust each other. You have to know we're not going to beat you or harm you in any way. We just need to work a few things out. I just don't understand why you did what you did to me. I guess I have to be obedient and follow God's way or I'm not going to be in His will."

Trav asked for forgiveness. He said he was sorry and that he wanted to pay me back.

I said, "Well, Trav, you probably can pay me back. I will let you because I think there should be consequences. Mine was the last car that you are going damage and that was the last trouble you're going to get into if I have my way. It was no coincidence that of all the cars in that parking lot, God allowed it to be my car to let you know that God loves you so much, that He can use me to get you to know Jesus. Most of my friends in Gig Harbor are Christians, too. Some of your punishment is going to be to pay us back for the tires. But also, you will be going to church with us and to youth group. (I'm one of the youth leaders.) I am involved in Sea Scouts, and you'll be going with me there, too. You are going to be under my care for the next couple of weeks.

He agreed to that even though he admitted he was a little bit scared.

Ron was standing back watching. He went up to shake hands with Trav and talked to him for a couple of minutes. Trav acted shy and embarrassed.

On the way home I was real curious as to why he would do this to my car. He said that he and his little friend were told by the dad to go out with the machete back to where the blackberry vines were and cut away at them. They were whacking on the vines between the house and the graveyard. This was to be their punishment from getting into trouble before. They got bored and decided to go across the highway to the fence where they leaned, debating over which car to put their knives into. I asked Trav, "Why did you do that?"

Trav told me that he had just joined a gang. Some of the rules were they had to jump off a high bridge into the water and swim so far. They had to climb the high school building and jump. Since he was deathly afraid of spiders, the gang filled his hands with them, and he had to squeeze them and kill them. They also required him to do damage to a certain number of cars within a certain length of time.

Together they talked over which car they were going to attack. Mine was the seventh car he would damage, choosing not to get the little red sports car. For some reason, they were drawn to my bronze colored Chrysler

New Yorker. Trav plunged his sharp knife into the front tire until it exploded, attracting the attention of passersby. The kids were chased until they ran out of sight.

On the way home to Gig Harbor he shared his adventures with the group. But, little did he know that he had picked the wrong car when he picked mine. He couldn't have known that I would have enough spunk to go after him and catch him. With God's help, I found him.

2
An Angel Unaware

It was a brisk day in Seattle when I opened the car door and stepped into the windy cool breeze. And yet, the sun was bright as I gave Bill a kiss and a hug before he left for his meeting downtown near the courthouse. He gave me $20, the only bill he had with him at the time, and the checkbook, telling me to go have fun while he went to his business meeting. We had just prayed about the day trusting God for whatever happened.

That morning we read about a big sale that was going to be at the Bon Marche. So I went there and found people standing in line at the door waiting for the store to open. Coming from a small town in Washington, I felt in awe of the city bustle amongst the tall buildings and the big city store windows. With Christmas around the corner, maybe I would find something.

As I stood in line, the 15th person back, I noticed both men and women, young and old people, from all branches of life. Some were quiet and subdued, some were talking and laughing. Since I was there by myself I was observing the crowd and taking everything in. For some reason, I didn't notice at first the little old black lady in a long brown wool coat. But, as I turned around and looked over my shoulder, I saw her coming towards me. I wondered "of all the people standing in line, why am I being approached?"

She walked directly towards me. Tugging at my coat sleeves, the little lady asked, "Do you have any extra money you could give me? I'm hungry and I need some food."

I quickly thought about the $20 that Bill gave me. Putting my hand in my pocket I gripped the money even tighter in my hand. I didn't have any change so I said, "I don't have anything smaller than a $20. That's all I have right now."

The little lady said, "Okay. Thank you." Then, she turned her back and started walking down the street.

I stood there wondering why I needed to compose myself. Feeling uncertain about my feelings, I took a deep breath. The deep breath suddenly turned into tears. As the tears began to roll down my cheeks I realized that I had not done the right thing. The experience with the little old lady happened so fast. I didn't understand why she chose me to ask for money. But what I didn't understand even more was why I had refused her. I was embarrassed for my tears so I got out of line and ran to the alley.

Once out of sight, and supported by the dirty brick wall of the adjacent building, I felt free to weep and cry out to God. "Oh, God, what was I supposed to do? I was supposed to feed her, and I didn't." Then I remembered what Jesus said, "When you feed the hungry, you are feeding me." I knew that to refuse the little old lady was to refuse God. With the encouragement I received from prayer, I lifted my head up and ran out of the alley to look for her. As I walked, I prayed. "Oh Lord, help me find the lady, and I can take her to breakfast."

I looked all around and couldn't find her at first. And then, I saw her crossing the street next to the Bon Marche. I ran to catch up with her, and this time *I* caught *her* by the coat sleeve.

"Forgive me!" I said. "Let me get change and take you to breakfast!"

"Oh, thank you!" said the little old lady. "There's a McDonald's around the corner."

I told her, "Oh good; we can go in there."

We went into the big McDonald's restaurant, and we sat down at the table. I told her my name. She said her name was Mrs. Brown and that she had been very sick. She was on welfare and out of food. Her daughter was coming from New York City that week to help her, so she just needed a little help temporarily.

I said, "That's fine. I'll be glad to help you." I asked her what she would like and went to place the order of eggs, toast and coffee. The young boy that took the order said to me "Oh, I see you know Mrs. Brown!"

"Well, not really! I just met her on the street. We came in for breakfast."

I needed to know more about her. The boy said, "She sure is a sweet lady. But, she's been very sick. Her daughter is coming to help her."

Reassured, I felt good that I was really helping someone in need, and not someone just trying a scam. I went back to sit down with Mrs. Brown. I asked if we could pray over the food.

Mrs. Brown said, "Yes. Yes. Let me." Bowing her head and taking my hand she thanked God for the food and for meeting me. She thanked Him for my obedience. Her beautiful prayer touched me in a way that made me know that Mrs. Brown was a Christian and that she knew the Lord.

I sipped hot chocolate as Mrs. Brown enjoyed her meal. Suddenly, I looked up to see a handsome, well-dressed middle-aged man in a long trench coat with matching hat. He was coming closer and closer towards us! "Oh my goodness." I thought.

I tried to not look at him by holding my head down. But, I felt his hand tap my shoulder. Looking up, I faced the man and saw his hazel colored eyes look straight at me. They were clear and sparkling. He had a big smile on his face. The man told me, "I thought I should let you know that I have been watching you all morning. I watched you get in line with all those people who were waiting for the store to open. I saw this little lady pass everyone else up and come directly to you. I heard her ask you for money. You told her that all you had was a large bill and didn't have any change. I even followed you when you ran into the alley and started crying."

I thought maybe my eyes were too full of tears to have seen him follow me. I listened to the man tell me, "I just want to bless you. That was such a sweet thing that you did." He lifted my hand up to put a wad of money in it.

Mrs. Brown sat watching with a smile on her face.

I pushed the chair back so I could stand up and speak to the man face to face. But he was gone! I asked Mrs. Brown who the man was, and she said she didn't know. I asked, "But, did you see him?"

Mrs. Brown said, "Yes, I saw him."

I asked, "Well, did you hear him?"

Mrs. Brown answered, "Yes, I heard him."

I asked again, "Well did you see what he did?"

"Yes. I saw that."

I put the money in Mrs. Brown's hand and said, "I don't know how much is here, but I know it's to bless you."

We both started to cry.

I told her "Well, I have some other things to do, and I've got to meet my husband at noon. I hope you'll be okay. I'll be pleased when your daughter gets here." We gave each other a big hug, then I left Mrs. Brown in the restaurant.

I ran across the street and down the block to the hotel where Bill was. As I ran into the building, he was just getting out of the meeting room. I asked him excitedly, "How'd your meeting go Bill?"

"Fine" he said. "How'd yours go?"

"Nothing that I expected happened. I didn't go shopping or anything that I intended to do, but I met this really neat lady and took her to breakfast. This angel of a man joined us!" I finished telling Bill the story. To this day, I still don't know who that man was or where he came from.

I don't know where he went. All I know is that I was really blessed that day and I learned a lesson that there really can be an "angel unaware."

3
The Run Away

I loved teaching art on KPTV 12 in Portland, Or egon. We always had a great time and loads of fun with my buddy and host, Rod Andrews. Nothing was ever very serious when Rod and I got together in front of the TV cameras. I always got tickled at some dumb thing he did or said. I usually started laughing at Rod and ended up doing something even more stu-

Rod Andrews, Delaney on KPTV Portland, Oregon

pid. The cameramen and crew joined us, and we were all out of control. We usually received loads of calls and mail. (I talked Rod into traveling with Bill and I. We were tour hosts around the world for years. Rod went with us several times to Jerusalem, Greece, Denmark, Jordan, Egypt, and other countries. There are so many wonderful stories to tell about our travels. But, later!)

One day after doing our TV show again we received a call came from Naselle's Boys' Correctional Institution. They asked if I could come and teach art once or twice a week. I've taught many people in many places, but never bad boys serving time. I loved working with kids at YMCA camp and traveling to different states teaching at church camps. Little did I know this adventure would change my life forever.

I remember the excitement in my heart at the thrill of a new adventure. As I drove onto the grounds, all was quiet, and there were few people wandering about. I noticed several large dorm type buildings (some with bars and all with big lock-in gates and doors.) I drove to the large art building and parked my car.

I started to unload my easel, paints, and other supplies. I looked up into the face of the most handsome young boy. He had big blue green eyes, long light brown hair and the biggest grin on his face from ear to ear. He introduced himself as Rich, 15-years-old, and said that he came to help me set up for class. What a big husky, tall strong youth for being so young.

I was nervous as he led me into a big room with at least 20 boys waiting. I was even more nervous when Rich picked up my large easel, aimed it at the other boys and pretended to mow them all down with his make be-

22

lieve machine gun easel. Some boys ducked, some shot back (pretend). About that time is when their supervisor Donna yelled for all to sit down and be quiet. To my surprise they did. I was then introduced as their new art teacher.

As the class was then all turned over to me, I started to silently pray! "God be with me and let you be in charge." As of now I was a bit scared (not too scared) because I knew who was on my side and He'll never let me down. I get in trouble, 'yes,' but not <u>down</u>! I explained what we were going to paint and just how. I then had Rich help me pass around the tubes of paint. I asked that he squeeze out on the palette papers paint for every 3 boys. First, Burnt Umber, Burnt Sienna, Yellow Ochre,

Some of the Harmond kids

and etc. As Rich started squeezing he started yelling that most of my paint looked like s____ (dung) and wasn't sure he wanted to mess with it. Well, I finally got all the boys to start painting and to follow me in mixing and strok-

23

ing. To my surprise most of the brats (and they were brats) could follow me and did a good job on their first painting. It was a beautiful Northwest mountain scene. They were even shocked with what they did.

Teachers and other counselors all came in to "ooh"

Some more of the Harmon kids

and "ahh." I had lunch with the boys and learned these kids were not little Boy Scouts. They had all gotten caught doing crimes I didn't know a 15-to-19-year-old could do. I had a lot to learn. My heart was broken as Rich told me he was in for stealing food for he and his little brother. His mom and step-dad were serving time in Oregon prisons, and the two boys were running wild. Rich was hard core and after serving his time he would have no real home to go to.

I had prayed all the way to Naselle from Longview (about a 2-hour drive). I prayed that God would use me and the talent he had given me to help these boys. Little did I know that I would be crying all the way home and be an emotional wreck. In my heart I wanted to be a mother to all the homeless boys I met that day. Right away I asked about taking Rich home. Naive me! I didn't know he would lie, cheat, steal, run away and at times be like a wild animal. All these boys were damaged, and I wanted to help fix them - starting with Rich.

I began having Rich on a day pass and then on weekends. Finally, Bill and I had him on weekends and holidays. All was going great until we were to get full custody of Rich. Not only did he run away, he got in trouble, was caught and put on a bus to be placed in a group home in Eastern Washington. There he was on the bus, and on his way from Naselle with money he had earned in his pocket. About half way on his journey he decided to go the other way. So again he was on the run. The officers called me to see if he had shown up back at our home (which he had always done before).

No one heard from him for weeks, and my heart was broken. I've never hurt over or loved someone else's son as I did this one. Bill and I prayed for this kid day and night for weeks, and then one day I received a phone call. It was Rich. He called every week, but wouldn't let us know from where. I kept receiving his calls over the next several months. One-day (while on the phone) he was surrounded by police, held at gunpoint, and taken in. Rich ended up in lock up at Green Hill Correctional Home for boys (a reform school).

I was allowed to visit Rich and finally able to give him private oil painting lessons behind bars. He not only painted well, but sold a lot of his work. Rich finally was released several years later and married. That also was a rocky road, but he was always close to Bill and I. Even today, we still get calls and visits from our first adopted juvenile delinquent.

Since then we have taken in dozens of other unwanted boys, and God has done wonders with these kids. It does take a village to raise a kid. We should all love and help our youth. With God's help these kids can and will make it out of life's refuse pile of humanity.

4
Shut Up and Paint!

Whad just arrived in Wilder, Idaho with our friends Steve and Dawn Gregg. This darling young couple had a music ministry and also hosted a local Christian TV. show.

Cheryl and Bob Heinrick from our former church had just moved to Wilder. They were now pastoring in a small church out in the country. They had asked the four of us to come visit and help with a service or two. Steve and Dawn had their program all together and knew what instruments they would play, songs to sing and had it all together. As for Bill and I? Yes, in my mind I knew just what we were going to do. Bill would read scripture, introduce me and I'd do my own thing, which was talking, telling stories and painting on anything that would stand still.

Months before we had a Pastor's Appreciation Sunday for our Pastor Gary Peters. Members with different talents were performing for God and Rev. Gary Peters. Some sang, some played different music instruments, danced, etc. For my talent that God had given me, I set up an easel, got out a large canvas and paints. Then right on the altar I gave Gary a free art lesson and an oil painting. I painted as fast as I talked and soon my Northwest mountain scene was done and given as my gift to Pastor Gary. He seemed very pleased and several in the service later asked me to do the same in other churches. Little did I know what we had started.

Delaney teaching on t.v.

That was how we ended up in Idaho. We were all set up that night and all ready, I thought. But, the next morning of all things and, for the first time in my life, I could not speak and had truly lost my voice. I was making a strange noise and became upset when I couldn't talk, yell, scream or anything as usual. Now what? In my strange sounds I let Bill know I could not speak. He was as shocked as anyone was and, at first, we laughed. Then I started crying.

Bill was so understanding and told me not to feel badly. We'd just explain to everyone what had happened, and maybe some other time I could come back and do my stories and paintings.

Then I did have a fit and went back into our guestroom. I fell across the bed sobbing and so disappointed in myself. I had sense enough to shut up and ask God why and what was I to do now? As I lay there feeling sorry for myself, I felt a feeling of comfort and could hear some inner voice telling me to open and start silently reading the Bible. As I opened the Bible I started reading the book of Genesis, "In the beginning God created the heavens and the earth."

Then I had the strangest thing happen. I heard Bill's voice reading, and I had a vision of me painting on a large canvas. It was a beautiful painting of God's creation,

Delaney and Margo Condon in KPHO studios Phoenix, Arizona

mountain, water, birds, trees, a small shepherd and sheep. God let me know I was to "shut up" and let Bill read the story of Genesis, Chapter 1 and 2. Together we could be God's team sharing his story. I wrote Bill a fast note and told him what just happened and asked if he thought we could do it. He smiled in his quiet gentle way and squeezed my hands and said, "let's go for it!" I wiped my tears and waited for our introduction to the gathering crowd with no practice and not sure what was happening. Bill told the people what had just happened. For the first time on stage we were acting as a team.

Bill asked all for a moment of prayer, and he prayed for blessings on what we were about to do, for my hands to paint for God's glory and for my voice. Then we began.

Bill read, and I painted what he read. The heavens, the earth, light across the sky, the sea, birds, trees, shepherd and animals and God's creations. It went so fast and so easy that I was shocked. I've never had my mouth so quiet in ever so long and all seemed to be enjoying it!

I finished putting in the final touches of my oil painting and held it up. The congregation started applauding and was in awe. Bill and I were also in awe, and we loved it. The painting was one of my better ones and it told the story of creation in full three-dimensional color.

God shut me up (for one day) and showed Bill and I what he wanted us to do and how to minister. Since that day we have traveled around the world and shared in almost 100 churches, Christian colleges and on TV.

I thank God for telling me to 'shut up and just paint with the talent he gave me.'

5
Who's in Our Garbage Can?

It was time to collect rent from our little apart ment complex. Bill does all the bookkeeping, but my part is to check on the renters and collect rent each month. As it was getting dark and starting to pour down rain, I grabbed one of our foster sons, John, to come along. We drove across town and parked in the carport in back of our rental units.

We headed for apartment #1 when I was stopped short by a strange noise coming from inside our Dempsey Dumpster (a large metal container the size of a small car.) I asked John to come with me and see what was making all that noise. One section of the large lid was up. I was sure we'd find a big cat, a stray dog or maybe a hungry opossum dining out. But to my surprise I found a little old man digging through our renter's garbage. The little man and I scared each other, and I asked him what in the world was he doing in there.

Embarrassed and not sure what to say, our newfound friend started trying to crawl out. John helped me pull the man out, and we stood staring at each other. I thought, "Oh! God, what do I do now?" My heart was heavy and I felt a sadness as I remembered all the kids and the adults we had fed, bathed and ministered to just weeks ago in the Mexico City garbage dump. But, here in Longview, Washington, USA I find a hungry person digging in our garbage. God have mercy!

We found the man was out of work, no money for food, his wife had died a few weeks ago and his mentally retarded older daughter just moved in with him. He was just looking for food to fix a meal.

A couple of our renters heard the noise we were making in the carport. Soon, several of us were in the carport wondering what to do. John looked at me and said 'Can we take him home and feed him? He can have my big T-bone steak we just bought for tomorrow's supper.' I put my arms around John and the little man and told him to get into my car. We would feed him a big healthy meal. Our renters who came out told me to bring our new friend back after we fed him. They had food to send home with him.

I forgot about collecting rent. I knew John and I had another duty to perform. We threw the dirty soiled bread and scraps all back in the garbage. I assured the man we'd get him fresh bread. We drove back to our big warm home on the hill. John ran ahead of us and started putting food on the table. We let the man wash up, and he sat at the table as John and I started cooking. What a friendly kind looking man we had found. He was old and worn, as were his clothes. We liked him and enjoyed his life story. We found his life was very sad, yet he had faith and knew God was always there for him. He gave God credit for us finding him.

6
Roses for the Garbage Dump

We were on the airplane headed for Mexico
City. Not just the city, but our time would
be spent mostly in the garbage dump.
Yes, the garbage dump! Not only with the garbage, rats
and the pigs, but also with the precious children and their
families. We knew they were living in cardboard boxes
and huts of old metal sheets for walls. It seemed unbelievable to us, but it was the only safe place after the 1985
earthquake. It destroyed so many of their homes, busi-
nesses and everything the people owned.

Only a few weeks ago my Bill and I were invited to
a Northwest Medical Team banquet in Longview, Washington. The invitation came from one of my art students
who was a nurse. We had no idea how that invite would
change our lives. They introduced us to a wonderful team
of people. Ron Post and his Northwest Medical Teams
send people of all trades and talents who are willing to do
God's work all around the world when there is need. They
serve and love the poorest of the poor.

My heart was broken after seeing films and meeting
others who work in the dumps around the world. My
eyes were full of tears and my heart was racing like crazy.

I looked at Bill and saw he was being touched the same as I was. We agreed that we had to go help. So we signed up as team leaders and asked 11 people to join us. Pastor Von Matthews gave us blessings and prayers, and we were off.

As we sat on the plane I found myself so excited and full of dreams and expectations. I knew, and so did my Bill, that when I get "hyper" I had best find something to keep me busy or else I get into trouble. I thought, "Lord, help!" So I pulled out a big roll of satin ribbon and started making ribbon roses. My Mom taught me to make roses back in the 1940's before plastic or silk flowers were created. I thought these would make nice Mother's Day gifts for the children to give their moms in the dump that following Sunday.

Children living in Mexico City garbage dump

As I got a dozen or so roses piled between Bill and me, I noticed two of the flight attendants were watching. They wanted to learn to make my roses. They also wanted to buy several! I told them they weren't for sale, but I would give them some. They insisted on paying me, and the next thing I knew other passengers wanted roses. Little did I know they were collecting dollar bills for each rose, and soon I had a lap full of bills. I thought "Oh! Great! Now I am

Harmonds worked in the Mexico City garbage dump on nine trips with the N.W. Medical Teams

going to be in trouble with Northwest Medical Team and the airlines for selling roses in the air." I didn't know it at the time, but God knew. He would later use these roses to rescue us from deep debt with the Mexican officials. I took all the bills and shoved them into Bill's pocket. Now he could be in trouble with me. I made roses all the way and kept passing them around the plane.

After we landed we had to pay for help getting all our 22 duffel bags out of the airport. The missionaries' little truck had no room for all 11 of us, our personal bags, and the 22 extra bags. We had to pay for several taxis to get us to Senior Ortez's home which was miles from the airport. We were told we must pay almost $100 to get our bags and us out of the airport!

None of us had extra money for this, but then I remembered the money I had stuffed into Bill's shirt pocket! In his pocket was exactly the dollar amount we needed to pay tips, taxes and the taxi drivers. Once again I learned that God was with us and could use my artwork for His Glory! When we're on God's team He is never a dollar short or a day late.

7
Bandits of the Towels

Today I ran across a Northwest Medical Team newspaper. In it I found a story of our trip to the Mexico City garbage dumps. The newspaper article was entitled, *"Los Banditos de Las Toallas"* or "Bandits of the Towels." (I recalled during the trip explaining to Ron Post, our NWMT President, that God had reminded me we needed towels.)

One of the activities our youth group from Gig Harbor performed included teaching basic hygiene. We had pooled our funds and brought along toothbrushes and toothpaste, bars of soap and some clothing – but we'd forgotten the towels! We soon realized this as we began to lay out our next day's activities. That evening, I thought 'Where can we get enough towels for all the kids? Who uses towels?' Then it occurred to me. We were only two blocks from a big hotel *loaded* with towels. I shouted to Bill and our team of 12 that we needed to head for the Sheraton Hotel and beg, borrow, or steal (just kidding) some towels for the children.

Off we went to see the managing director of the Sheraton. Having been forewarned of our visit, he was under the impression we were a group of disgruntled tourists, unhappy with our accommodations.

We had to pass the American Embassy on our way. The whole block was surrounded with soldiers armed with heavy machine guns and armor because of the poverty, theft and terrorism. As I walked in front of a group of the young men, I remembered I had a bag of big American lollipops in my backpack. I greeted the young men and asked if they would like an American treat. They all said 'gracias' as I passed the candy around the block. Bill asked me what in the world was I doing that for? I laughed and said I was sure they wouldn't shoot me.

Mexico City children wrapped in hotel towels and bath robes

Little did I know we could have been shot later by sneaking out the back underground garage with the 50 new towels we were just given. (The Sheraton's managing director was so relieved and excited about the real purpose of our visit, he not only agreed to help, but was extremely generous!)

The managing director explained that people had been caught stealing from the hotel, so he asked Bill and

I to lead our group down the garage and sneak out the back. He didn't want others to see us in the lobby and walking out the busy front doors all loaded with new towels. But, we were seen. The men to whom I had just given the suckers were just across the street from where we were sneaking out. At first several soldiers approached

Amy, Sara, and Bill Harmond in Mexico City garbage dump with N.W. Medical Team

us and then remembered we were the missionaries that had just given them all the lollipops. They relaxed their guns, greeted us and helped us across the heavy traffic. As an American, you don't want to be arrested in Mexico. Thank you God for the candy and for the towels!

(NOTE: The next summer we visited, The Sheraton Hotel not only saved towels for us, but they had pretty pink maid dresses for each mom in the dump. These we gave out on Mothers' Day. Again and again God provides.)

8
Old Lady in the Cardboard Box

Today I was to head home from a wonderful two weeks of working with the children in the Mexico City garbage dump. This was my second trip to Mexico City. A few months ago we were on our very first trip with the Northwest Medical Team. We started building a new medical clinic right on the edge of the city dump. We fed, clothed and ministered to people living in garbage piled as high as 70 feet. We found families living and eating with the rats and pigs. Our hearts were broken after our first visit there, and I knew I had to come back. It's very exciting for me to realize that God can use each and every one of us if we let him know we're available.

I went home from our first trip remembering the smell and sights of filth the Mexican children were living in. You cannot believe it until you see, smell, feel and step into this unfamiliar world. I just knew I had to go back and bathe and love those beautiful children.

It had been a wonderful rewarding two weeks. I would never forget my awaking dream just last night. I was spending my last night with Lolo's mother and father-in-law. Lolo was our Northwest Medical Team's head missionary in charge of the children's ministry in the dump.

I had a dream that Jesus was in my bedroom. He told me that I was to leave most of my clothes for someone in the garbage dump where I had been the past two weeks. I had given out duffel bags full of children's clothes and shoes and some grown-up clothing. Why was I to give away my own clothes? I was wide-awake at 3:00 a.m. Jesus seemed so real in my room.

I jumped out of bed and opened my suitcase that I had neatly packed a few hours before. There were five nice tops, two pairs of new slacks, two dresses, two long skirts, work jeans and shoes. And, my beautiful new sweater. I had paid more than usual for this nice cardigan sweater for the chilly airplane ride and for evenings at home in the rain. Selfishly, I thought that perhaps my clothes would be a bit big for any small Mexican lady in the dump. Even though I love bright colors, my clothes are modest, and perhaps they wouldn't fit anyone. I didn't really want to, but I pulled out all my clothes, except for a skirt and blouse to wear home. (We always leave our work clothes and shoes in the dump as they get so soiled.) I placed my clothes in a sack and went back to sleep.

At 8:00 a.m. sharp Lolo came by to pick me up for my last few hours in the garbage dump. We would teach Bible study and feed the kids breakfast. As we headed out, I told Lolo of my dream and that I had most all my clothes, including my new sweater to give away. I told Lolo that I had no idea why the dream and who would get my clothes. .

He stopped the car, started laughing, and gave me a big hug. Lolo and I have always gotten along and love each other because we have the same love for the children, Jesus and for others. Often he and I would be thinking of doing and sharing the same things at the very same time. It was no surprise when he told me Jesus had spoken to him also that night. He was told to go back to the dump and that someone needed his help. It was raining and very late as Lolo drove back to the dump site. He then started, walking along the dirt trail that led between the tin and cardboard shacks. Way down near the end of the winding path Lolo heard someone crying in the distance. He came upon a large cardboard box all covered with old rags. Inside he found a little old grandmother all dirty, wet and hungry. She had no one to care for her and had become too ill to care for herself. She was so thrilled to see Lolo. She told him she had prayed that someone would hear her prayers, her crying and rescue her.

Lolo carried her back through all the trash and clutter and up on the hillside to a friend's warmer shack. The shack had dirt floors and old mattresses and bedding where her friend and Lolo put her to bed. They fed her and asked if she needed anything else. The old lady was so thankful for all the help already given, but she so wanted some clean clothes and especially a warm sweater.

It always amazes me how and when God works, and who and what he uses to answer one of his children's prayers. Lolo gave my clothes to the precious old lady. They were a perfect fit.

Arriving back in Gig Harbor, with my almost empty suitcase, I marveled at how beautiful, green and oh so clean is our charming Gig Harbor. We Americans do live in a different world. No matter how many trips we make overseas we always have to be deprogrammed and given time to resettle in our own space.

My home is so beautiful and so full of material things that the people I had just left would never see or have. I found myself crying as I watched my washing machine fill with clean hot water and lots of soap to wash the three large loads of clothes. Yesterday I had bathed dozens of kids with no change of clothes. Why are we so blessed to be born in America?

I was excited to be back home and to get ready for a big art show the next weekend. About fifty of us artists were invited to put on an art show at Harbor Plaza shopping mall in Gig Harbor. The show was a big success. I always enjoyed demonstrating my oil painting and meeting the public. All seem to enjoy an artist in action show. I had invited my friend Carol Hall and her wonderful art work all from Bible stories. We were placed on the sidewalk in front of Fran Nickleson's shop, Fashions First. During the show several merchants had a drawing for us artists. We all signed up and waited to see who would be blessed with all the neat gifts.

That next Monday after our show I received a call from Fran that my friend Carol Hall had won first prize in the mall drawing. She wanted me to call Longview and give Carol the good news. I was thrilled that Carol had won the gifts from Fashions First. It included a gift certificate and a beautiful scarf, earrings and a pink cardigan sweater. I called Carol and told her the good news. She started laughing and said she knew days ago that she had won. I said how could you? They just drew the names today. She then informed me that as she signed her name on the drawing entry, a strange thing happened.

Carol said she heard a voice telling her she had already won the drawing and that she was to bless Delaney (me) with all the gifts. She also didn't know why, but was sure God was telling her that this was to be a blessing for me. I started crying, as I knew Carol could really use the gifts. I told Carol I couldn't accept them. She yelled at me, "If you don't take this from me, then you'll cheat me out of other blessings God has for me." She told me to shut up and go get my new sweater and other things. I asked her if she knew I had just four days before given my clothes and new sweater away in the Mexico dump. She laughed and said 'No, but God knew all along.' As Bill had said, "you can't out give God."

9
Fingerprints on My Roses

Here we were, ministering in the Mexican garbage dump again. We were always surprised and blessed to find what God had for us. On this trip, I received the most precious gift. Our Northwest Medical Team helped build a new medical clinic, feed, bathe and clothe the children.

I had just taught a class for the children and painted a large oil painting for them. As we packed up to leave,

Getting paintings ready for television show

some of the women presented me with a lovely bouquet of handmade, long stem, pink roses. I couldn't believe how they were made, and I began to cry. The women had collected old white bread from the garbage dump, to this, they mixed old bottles of Elmer's Glue, reused red hair dye and ounces of glycerin. They shaped this mixture into beautiful, single, rose petals. They then molded and shaped these into beautiful rose buds and full roses. The roses were then set in the hot sun to bake. The women found wire and green tape and created this wonderful bouquet for me.

I am still blessed each time I look at my precious gift. For there on each rose petal is a unique fingerprint form of each woman. I felt so loved that day and had no idea what a wonderful God-given talent these women had.

Again, I found that we can never out-give God!

10
God's Blue-Eyed Bird

"Today is the day the Lord has made and be glad in it!" Not today, I thought, could I be glad. One phone call and we had word that one of our youth pastors was leaving our church because of terrible rumors. I had also just received word that another dear friend didn't want to live anymore and was so alone and rejected. "How could I be glad in this day?" I was asking God as I wrapped a big dry towel around my hair, slipped into a long robe and stepped out on our deck outside.

What a wonderful view. There was the great Puget Sound, Point Defiance and that unbelievable beauty of Mount Rainier. The air was fresh with the smell of salt water, and the sound of seagulls. What a sight to behold and right here from our very own deck. We were so blessed and had so much to be thankful for.

It wasn't but a few months ago that God had moved us and taken such wonderful care of us. I began crying out to God for protection and blessings for our two friends we had just heard from. One was from Longview, Washington and the other from Denver, Colorado. I knew God heard us and touched us wherever we are in this world.

My heart was filled with sadness, and I began to weep. As I lifted my arms toward the sky, I begged for God to hear me and let me know he was near. I reached out to let my Abba Father know I needed him. I closed my eyes and asked God to let me know he was with my friends. Sometimes God answers right away and some times it can take forever, but again today my Heavenly Father was right there with me.

I was listening to the seagulls and the wonderful sounds that the ocean provides and all of a sudden I heard the flapping of wings and felt a cool breeze whistling around me. Dropping out of the sky, there was a beautiful black bird (so black he glowed of blue) and of all things,

he had beautiful shiny blue eyes. Suddenly he stopped in mid-air and landed on my arm. He sat staring up at me! At first I couldn't believe what had just happened and was wondering just where my new little friend had come from. Then I thought 'maybe

God's blue eyed bird

he's just another wonderful gift from God.'

I realized I had better get dressed, and on my way to my morning meeting. I stroked the beautiful feathers on the bird's back and expected him to fly away. But, there he stayed on my arm. I walked into the house and as I opened the door the bird flew in ahead of me! I went into the bathroom to brush my teeth. As I ran the water into the sink the bird flew right under the flowing water and started bathing himself. He ducked his head, dipped his wings and danced around in the water. I then plugged in my hair dryer to dry my hair and he jumped out of the sink and landed on the counter top. There he spread his wings and sat there letting his wings flap in the air from my dryer as his feet stood firm.

I watched him with wonder and asked this funny little guy if he wanted to be hair dried now that he had his bath? He lifted his wings even higher as I aimed the warm hair dryer under his wing. He loved it and danced in a circle in order to absorb all the warm air he could. I started laughing out loud fully enjoying this amazing bird. My hair was still wet and droopy, but his feathers were now all nice and dry. The fluff on his tummy and under his beak was all fluffy. His feathers were bright and shiny. I finished drying my hair and watched as he spread his wings and flew up on our shower curtain. There he lit, looked at me, winked his eye, and tucked his head under his beautiful feathers and fell sound asleep.

Now what should I do? I had to leave and I tried to get my feathered friend out of the house and back out side. But, there was no way he was going to leave his sleeping perch. I got dressed, bid him good bye and closed the bathroom door. I wasn't sure what Bill would think when he came home and found a strange jet-black bird with blue eyes sitting on the shower curtain. Bill *was* surprised and not sure where he came from. He couldn't get the bird outside either so just left him stay inside.

Later, I got a big birdcage and put him inside and man, did he have a fit! He all but screamed and jumped up and down 'til I let him out. He then lit on the outside of the cage and there he stayed. He even wanted to eat outside his new cage. I called my friend, Janet Robertson, to come see our new-feathered friend. Bill and I even took him to church Sunday morning. He flew around inside the lobby and wouldn't go outside for a minute. He'd always find me and land on my head or shoulder. We took videos of him and all his crazy doings.

Weeks later we were to leave for Mexico City again to check on and work with the children living in the garbage dump there. We left our bird now named "Solomon" with our friends on a nearby farm.

To this day we know not from where our "Solomon" came, but we do know that in my sadness and among my tears, God brought a lot of laughter and fun! He gave us a beautiful blue-eyed bird.

11
Five More Jamaicans

We were on a return visit to Jamaica at Christ for the Nations College. Bill and our team from Gig Harbor were all out buying paint and supplies to paint and build around the campus.

Being the artist that I am, I have a desire to paint and teach all the students that I can. The students have breaks and extra time during the day. When we visit, I always set up a large table of painting supplies right outside our guestroom and on the beautiful patio overlooking Montego Bay. On this trip I brought dozens of blouses, shirts and hats to paint for the campus gift shop. This project helps pay students' college tuition and is so rewarding. I had learned from earlier years not to teach the young gardeners and other hired help during working hours. (I had done that on our first trip.) I was excited to have the hired help learn to paint and get new clothes and yes! I got yelled at!

This trip (about our 8th) I knew to teach the helpers on their lunch hour. In the middle of art class I started asking about six of the young men of their walk with Jesus. To my surprise most did not know Him. I found out a couple of the young men were living with a mate, not married and had children. Very common in Jamaica, about 85% have children and unmarried. That is why CFTN is so important with their Christian training.

A dashing 80 year old lady, Elsie Connell taught Janet and I to make homemade soap. She sends thousands of bars around the world

The young men working on the grounds were un-educated and very poor. I thought they needed to know Jesus and I would teach them right then. So we had a Bible study. I asked if they wanted to accept Jesus and five of the six said 'Yes, and now, today.' I didn't want to get into trouble again, so I ran and got the boss, Hank, and also the crew leader. I told them I was surprised these young men were not saved and it was about time. I led the young guys under the big mango tree. Then we knelt and prayed. I asked Hank to share also and help me lead them in the sinners' prayer. I knelt down, looked into these young men's big black eyes and saw the tears stream-ing down their beautiful dark cheeks. I couldn't help but weep and was so overcome with God's presence.

About that time Linford, the young student from Guyana, was just getting out of class and came walking by. He saw Hank and I on our knees, with me crying, and Linford knew for sure I had gotten in trouble again with Hank. He was sure I was crying because I was in *deep* trouble! He came running over and put his arms around me. He was so afraid of what I might have done this time.

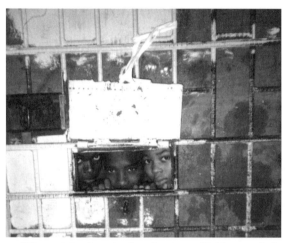

Harmond Team visits Jamaica boys' prison. Children picked up for stealing food (85% of the children have unmarried parents)

You see, he knew the day before I had thrown a big plate of food scraps and a bowl of Jell-O over the balcony. I knew the large white geese below were hungry, so I fed them. Well, the Jell-O melted in the hot heat and as I threw it, the bright red liquid Jell-O dumped and poured all over their white feathers. Just then Hank came by and was shocked to see all his white geese were now a bright pink. He knew immediately who was guilty and yelled at me for painting his geese.

I quickly explained to Linford that I wasn't in trouble this time and told him all we were doing under the mango tree. Linford then knelt and prayed with us. What a thrill: five more beautiful Jamaicans for Jesus!

12
Tornado Night of Terror

Bill and I had just received word that we had won a trip to Florida and a cruise to the Bahamas! We're always half-packed and ready to go wherever the Lord sends us. Being a tour host and hostess around the world for 20 years was more than exciting! We never knew what was down our next path of life's adventure.

We had an uneventful flight from Seattle to Orlando. We got our rent-a-car and headed for our hotel located in the little town of Kisseme, Florida. It was late as we got settled in. Little did we know, we were settled in just a few blocks from where a horrible tornado had just landed.

The next morning on the TV news, the newscasters were asking for volunteers to come and help the Red Cross and Salvation Army. Our hearts were broken as we saw all the damage, destruction and lost lives.

I wasn't sure what Bill would think of us spending some of our vacation checking in with the Salvation Army or Red Cross to do what we could to help. We had several days before our ship left. But, not only did Bill want to help physically, he suggested we give them all the money we were going to spend on sightseeing and Disney World.

We called the news station and found out that the Salvation Army and the Red Cross were setting up teams in a large warehouse on the fairgrounds. The team leaders were thrilled and surprised that a couple from Gig Harbor, Washington would show up to help out. They were so organized and had telephones, computers and equipment all ready. We were asked to sort water, medicine, food and clothing, into family packs which were then loaded into trucks and distributed to the people in need.

Among the other volunteers, were three young men on vacation from New York. They were all free for two weeks and had made no real vacation plans. They had seen on TV the great damage in Orlando. All three worked in construction and knew they could be used. So, they, too, spent their vacation helping others in need. What a blessing they were!

Before they left on a construction crew, these three young men helped me unload a large box. As we pulled the lid back on the box, we found letters, pictures, love notes and written prayers to the survivors of the Tornado. This box of new clothing and kids things came from a classroom many states away. We all had tears running down our faces as we sorted out the letters to put into each family pack.

We saw so much damage and sights we had never seen before during our 'vacation.' One little guy will have a story to tell when he grows up. The tornado had splintered his wood frame home and grabbed 18-month-old Jonathan. But, the deadly twister seemed to have a change of heart when confronted with a child. The same winds snapped off the top of a nearby Oak tree and deposited him in its protective branches. There the baby lay, nestled safely in his mattress, while around him the world seemed to be coming to an end.

Time flew as we were busy sorting many supplies, clothes, medicine, food and a bit of everything. Most of the world had heard about the deadly tornado and had responded with compassion. It was wonderful how God had touched the hearts of so many and how His people had come to help the survivors.

———————

It was lunch time, and we were asked to line up and serve ourselves. 'My goodness,' I thought, 'Where did all this wonderful food come from?' There was fried chicken, cornbread, ribs, ham, all kinds of wonderful sandwiches, vegetables and lot of homemade dishes and goodies. What a feast! I was hungry (as always) and could hardly wait to eat. Bill wasn't ready to stop working and said he felt we shouldn't be eating their food. I had to let him know it was specially cooked and brought in for all the helpers. I fixed him a plate, and he hesitantly ate with me. Again, I was shown the unselfishness in my Bill.

While in the food line, I met a darling older woman who was volunteering on the Red Cross side of the large warehouse. She asked me to look at the busy 10-year-old boy talking on the phone across from us. I looked up and stared at the darling Mexican boy. He was talking so fast and so seriously. Not only was he talking with his mouth, but with his hands. He was standing up and waving and using his arms with every word. The lady proceeded to tell me that the boy (Joe was his name) had come to the warehouse early that morning (way before Bill and I). The lady started crying, as she finished telling me that little Joe came in to help other victims of the deadly tornado. His home had been destroyed and nothing left. The wonder of it all was this, the mother, father, two dogs and Joe's pet bird, were all found alive. He was so thankful and wanted to help others not so blessed. He wanted to work as a phone interpreter as he spoke fluent Spanish and English.

I'm sure God was pleased with little Joe on that day.

13
Jesus in the Mall

I had just heard that my missionary friends, Gary and Carol Hall, were headed to Japan. Carol did wonderful artwork detailing the life of Jesus. Her paintings showed Jesus in action today and in years past. Her work had a message for everyone. It so happened that our Tacoma Mall was having a big art show, and Carol was having her artwork there for the week. (I was expecting to see my friend and, because I was not in this show, I had time to watch her painting.)

Carol was easy to find in the center of the mall, painting under a large sign "The King's Paint Brush." She was surrounded by the only Christian paintings and Bible stories in the show. I was going to help watch and sell her art for the next two hours. The mall was crowded with people of all sizes, shapes, dress and color passing by. I prayed that God would bless Gary and Carol, and that He would allow me to be a blessing to them for this short time. People of all ages started slowing down to take notice of God's word. I did sell several paintings and prints.

Just then something happened that made me proud to be a Christian, and I knew Jesus was in the mall. Carol had painted a large picture of Jesus being nailed to the cross by Roman soldiers. There was pain in his eyes and blood streaming from his wrist as the heavy nails are hammered into them. I noticed a handsome young black man who looked like a kid to me. He was about 19 years of age. As I walked closer to him, I noticed he was lost in that painting, tears in his eyes. In a soft voice, unusual for me, I asked if I could help him or if he had any questions. He looked up at me and said the painting touched him. He was feeling the pain within it. I asked if he knew Jesus and, he said 'Yes,' but not as his personal savior. I asked if he wanted to know him personally. He said, "Yes!" I asked if I could introduce him to Jesus by having him give his life and his all to Jesus right then. I asked, "Are you ready? Jesus is always ready for you!"

"Yes!" he cried and, right there in the mall, in front of God and many others, we bowed our heads and prayed. After the sinner's prayer and one big hug, he asked if he could run to the nearby phone and call his mom. He called Mississippi to tell his Christian mom. She had prayed for that moment for years! We both stood by the phone weeping and rejoicing because Jesus was truly in the mall that day.

14
God Has A Plan for Dan

It was 2:00 a.m. when I was awakened by a dull tapping noise that wouldn't go away. Little did I know it was Cammy, a gutsy and daring 17-year-old who was trying to wake our foster son, Rick. I went to the back door, out over the patio, and there I found Cammy throwing rocks at Rick's bedroom window. I yelled, "What in the world are you doing?"

Cammy started to run and I, in my nightgown, ran after her. I caught her and asked, "Who are you? What do you want? And, *what* are you doing?"

She told me between short gasping breaths that she was a friend of Rick's. They had just met at the skating rink that night. Her dad, a state policeman, and mom were out of town for several days. She was bored, liked Rick from her first glance, and decided to get to know him better at 2:00 in the morning.

I had different ideas, and marched her into the house, put her on a spare bed and dared her to leave. I told her I would see her in the morning.

Cammy and I became really fond of each other and even though I usually don't work well with girls, this one

I learned to love. She was wild and crazy fun and always laughing, usually at me!

One day, Cammy brought home a darling handsome young 18-year-old by the name of Dan for me to meet. This kid was a doll with bright beautiful brown eyes, dark wavy brown hair and a smile from ear to ear. As I looked at Dan I suddenly realized that this was the grown 12-year-old who came into my YMCA art class years before. (I was the Art Director at the Longview YMCA for years.)

I remembered when this young boy walked into my art room and watched me teach oil painting to my students and didn't want to leave. Later he brought his mom to meet me. It seemed his mom had been married several times and wasn't around much. The boy hung around the YMCA and always ended up in my crowded art room. We found the he couldn't afford a membership, but my boss, Bob Rossi, and I gave Dan a scholarship for one year. He became quite an artist and never missed a class. His high school years were a bit rough, and he was off and on with his mom. Family life wasn't good.

Dan spent lots of time at our home and, as he grew older, he was a good witness to our wild foster boys. Bill and I claimed Dan as our own. More than once he helped to chase down a run away boy and bring them to our home. After high school Dan moved to California to work and live on his own. A year later, Dan showed up on our doorsteps and we were so pleased to see our old friend.

One night Dan was uneasy and concerned about where he was headed in life. He started to cry and ask if we could go for a drive and talk. We drove and talked as we had done since he was twelve. Finally I suggested that he give his life completely to the Lord and ask God to lead him. As we prayed together, I got the bright idea from 'you know who'. Yes! I'm sure it was God's idea not mine. I felt I should take Dan over to visit our doctor's daughter and her son. The daughter and I were good friends, and I knew she'd enjoy meeting Dan. Little did I know Dan would fall in love with her young son of about seven-years-old. The son was mentally retarded and had the sweetest spirit within him. He was thrilled to meet Dan and took him outside to swing, play ball and play games. Hours later, I had to pull the two boys apart as we headed for home. Before going to bed, we all prayed together and asked for guidance for Dan's life.

Dan had tears in his eyes as he told us he knew what he wanted to do. God had spoke to his heart that night and told him to teach the young. I asked if this meant he wanted to become a schoolteacher. He told us even the world "teacher" was beginning to excite him.

Early the next morning, I told Dan the Lord reminded me that my friend at the Christian Church needed young grads to train for teaching the little ones in their grade school five days a week. We called the church school and my friend Ruth told me to bring Dan right over. She hired him that day!

To shorten my story, he trained and taught and did so well that Ruth and the church helped send Dan to college where he received his teaching degree. He is now teaching on the military base in the Philippines. We see Dan when he comes back for summer breaks. He's so happy doing exactly what God had planned for his life. I hope some day our little mentally retarded friend will realize how important he was in a young man's life.

15
Gang Rags for Jesus

I worked for years at the Longview Church of God Youth Camp in Longview, Washington. One summer, I met and worked with the head National Youth Director, Reverend Keith, from California.

He took me home with him to work with the young convicts and troubled kids from his state. What a wonderful adventure and so many lives changed! We were able to lead many troubled kids to the Lord and to have them baptized.

We met kids who came to camp to do away with other gangs they knew were going to be there, and to harm us leaders. We had "altar calls" and asked the kids to bring forward all things on them that Jesus would not approve of. Wow! Girls came to the altar, pulling razor blades they had hidden in their hair (so when in a fight and someone grabs their hair, they would get their hands sliced up). Some of the boys brought up weed (marijuana), weird pipes, knives, blades, weapons, pills of all sorts and things I wasn't sure what they were.

The most wonderful sight I saw was the leader of a

"Crypts" gang and the leader of the "Bloods" crying their eyes out. I went over to pray for them. Right there, they both gave their lives to the Lord. I watched in wonder as they looked into each others' eyes and reached out to hug

Youth and young convicts being baptised at California Bible Camp

one another. We saw that same thing, night after night. Soon over a hundred youths were saved.

We had youth pastors from all over California and matched each kid with a church in their hometown. Some of the boys had a choice from the courts to attend our youth camp or go straight to jail because of crimes they had committed. I always looked forward to teaching at the high school youth camps and now have a collection of gang scarves, called "Rags."

In order to below to a gang, you must earn your colors. You are then given a colored scarf to wear and to show your membership and ownership of certain turf you protect. Initiation is to fight other members and run through a beating and whipping line up. Some of the initiations are almost unbearable. This shows how tough and what guts you have to become a member.

With God's help, I hope to collect dozens more. It is not good for the gang members to give up their colored rags and could mean death. We, as Christians, know that it means life forever when they turn their colors in for Jesus.

16
Garage Sale Tears

Everyone loves a bargain and a great garage sale. I'm no exception. But, most of all, I love meeting all the colorful people that come. Several times a year we collect and gather up any and everything for our mission sales.

I'm always amazed at what sells. Late this summer I had a wonderful sale and found myself even selling Jesus in my garage! You never know when or where he'll show up.

It was Saturday morning and cars began arriving. Up drove a nice big car, with a Grandma, aunt and a beautiful young mother with her two teenage children. I greeted them and asked if I could help them. They saw my big poster of our Mexico City garbage dump pictures. They saw 70 feet of garbage that the children, rats, pigs and dogs were living in.

I could tell the young mother was touched as she asked all about our mission work. We talked about our taking in other lost and hurting boys right here. She asked us what we do with kids that run wild and have no respect for a single mom or any adult authority. She then began crying and asked if I could pray for her and her family.

About that time, her daughter, a pretty young girl about 13-years-old, came and sat down beside me. The aunt and Grandmother were shopping around the pile of brand new things we had on the lawn. The mom said she wanted me to meet her son who she loved so much, but had lost complete control of. Out of their car jumped this young 15-year-old boy named Jonathan. He had a strange look as he said to me, "I know you. You're one of the youth leaders over at that Vineyard Church."

I laughed and said, "Yes! That's me!" He danced around and made some smart remark. I looked him in the face and said "If you don't behave, you'll end up here and be one of our kids."

He laughed and said, "Hell no, not me." Then I knew here was our next kid.

The family had just moved in down the street, and I had seen this boy skate-boarding late at night and even into the morning. I learned this kid runs from Tacoma, Gig Harbor and all around all hours of the night and had gotten into trouble. Seems a lot of his time had been spent in Remann Hall youth detention.

Jonathan was a cutie, and I always wondered (and still do) just how that skinny frame of his body could hold up all those yards of baggy pants. Then there are the four giant pockets sewn on the front and back of each pant leg. The crotch sags down to the knees. The wide shaggy cut hem of the pants drags behind on the ground. This kid would make a cute cartoon character. With his shaved head, except for the long blond curls hanging over his eyes from the very top of his head. This is a fashion state-ment? (Later in the week I ran across Jonathan and could hardly recognize him. He had dyed his head bright beet red and had dye around his ears, face, and dripping down his hands.)

Jonathan's mom spent ever so long talking with her daughter and me. We all three had tears in our eyes and prayed together that God would protect her children and help her start a new life in Gig Harbor. We became friends from that day on. She started going to our church, and God did change her life. Her daughter moved in with the Grandmother and Grandfather and seems to be doing great.

Jonathan got into more trouble and ended up in court, and Bill and I were given custody of him. Here I'd told the brat that first day I met him that he'd be our kid and so he is! We love this boy, but he's a tough one. I can't wait to see what God has planned for him. We'll wait and see what it is!

17
Beer for the Slugs

Here we are heading for the streets of Tacoma on another Friday night to feed the homeless and the poor. Todd, Ken, Regina and Beska have been going with me lately, and we've all been blessed. We take gallons of milk to pour as others bring hot soup, chili, sandwiches, fruit, etc. We line up card tables along the sidewalk and feed the hurting, homeless and lost people. We also give out shoes, clothes, blankets and more to keep them warm on cold nights on the streets, under the bridges. Wherever they can find.

Sometimes we see fights, drunkenness, drugs and sad things to behold. Last week I gave bowls of soup and clean jackets to two young men in exchange for the big full bottles of beer they had hidden from the police as their old beat up car was towed away. I took the beer home, poured it in pans around my garden and used it as slug bait. They crawl into the pans and drink and kill themselves in the beer.

I've seen humans do the same as the slugs. What a shame, and what a waste. Others are shocked to see all I have collected on the streets and what I'm able to pour out. But God knows it's no good and he'd pour it out, too.

18
God Provides

I was out in our garage cleaning up the melted mess of food from our defunct freezer. It seems it totally pooped out while we were away for several days. We came home to find a melted, stinky mess awaiting us. I was praying that insurance would cover all our ruined and spoiled food. Then I prayed for another refrigerator with a freezer to replace what we had just lost.

Later that day as I was cleaning out our closets at home, I found we were blessed with so much we never use. I knew the orthopedic thrift shop always needed donations to sell. I loaded up my car and headed to our little Gig Harbor shop. As I was busy unloading, I noticed I was very early, and there was no one around. All was quiet as I place my boxes under the little shed. All of a sudden a car drove up behind me and a middle-aged man came running up to me and asked if I could help him.

It seems he was all loaded up and leaving Gig Harbor to a new job back East. He asked if this little shop could take a nice running refrigerator. At the time, we so needed another refrigerator for our garage, not to mention all the extra food for our foster boys and all the food we take on the streets on Friday nights to feed the poor. I was so excited as he asked if I could please take it. (Our thrift shop won't take big appliances.)

The man asked me to follow him home to see what he had no room for on his moving truck. There I found a beautiful refrigerator with a long freezer compartment. He thanked me for helping him, and I called my Bill to come over to carry the freezer home. The man also gave Bill a nice big wheelbarrow and several other items. I offered to pay for all the gifts he gave us, but he said no. We thanked him and prayed for his safe journey.

Once again, I had found we cannot 'out give' God. I went to give a few boxes and came away more blessed than ever in the early morning at the thrift shop.

19
Josh for Jesus

It was early Tuesday morning. I was hurrying to
get out the door for Bible study which started at
Chapel Hill in half an hour. Ding-dong went the
doorbell. I ran to the door and there stood a handsome
young man in his fireman's uniform. I screamed, "JOSH!"
and grabbed him with a big hug. This young man, years
ago, was my crew-mate on the wonderful Sea Scout boat
named *The Odyssey*. (She was 90 feet of pure beauty and
wonderful adventure, designed as a training ship for the
youth who love the sea and wonders of sailing.) I had
watched Josh grow from a sassy 14-year-old on the boat
to the 20-year-old young rookie fireman standing before
me.

He was on his way home from fireman training and
decided to check on us as he pulled off the freeway in Gig
Harbor. I was torn between Bible study and my friend
Josh. Oh' what to do! I grabbed Josh and said, "Come
on! Please join me in our Bible study. The women will
love you!"

We drove to Chapel Hill just in time for class. I
introduced Josh to a few of the women, and we sat down
to hear our leader, Joanne Williams. Later I learned she

saw me enter the room with the young fireman. She was sure he was checking out the brand new building and the propped open fireproof doors in our meeting room that should not have been propped open. She slowly moved by the door and kicked it closed. She noticed the young fireman said nothing and was relieved she hadn't gotten into trouble.

Joanne started her teaching, and the first thing she shared was that for years she knew Jesus in her head, but not in her heart. She explained how wonderful it was to really know Jesus in your heart. Josh touched my hand and said "Delaney, that's just how I feel. I really need to know who God is, and I'm not sure I do." Later in our class, I felt the hurt and loneliness in Josh's heart.

Josh had just seen and experienced what real life and death was being a young fireman. He said it hurt so deeply after a night on duty. Sometimes after seeing death, he needed someone to pour his heart out to. Today he had chosen me to share with.

Josh said I could share with the Bible Study group what he was feeling and telling me. We asked Josh to share his story. I asked if he would like to give his life and all back to Jesus. With his hands shaking and with tears of joy, Josh prayed with me, the sinner's prayer. He rededicated his life to the Lord.

Wow, I really threw our Bible study off! But, the women thanked me for bringing Josh and wrote this little note in the next week's newsletter:

Women's Bible Study of Chapel Hill

Praise God:

For the rookie fireman that visited us and rededicated his life to Christ on November 18, 1997.

For the women that showed him the love of Christ.

For Delaney's boldness in bringing him.

I wasn't sure how Josh would react to all this attention from all these women, the write-up, and my telling his story. He said it was great. He began praying for his crew and all the hurting ones he's helping to save and to rescue on duty.

Chapel Hill thanked me for boldness in bringing Josh to an all women's Bible study, but I thank God for the boldness Josh had in going with me.

20
The Transformation
of Big Jeff

One Sunday morning, I was in a big hurry (as usual), and I ran through the church door. I wasn't looking where I was headed and "bong," I hit something big, hard and dark brown. As I pulled back from what I had just run into, I looked up and there he was. A handsome, but very angry and mean-looking, 6-foot-4-inch, 225 pound, 17-year-old, young man. I was stunned for a second and, without thinking (as usual), I said "Oh, my goodness! Whose brat are you?" Then I saw his big, dark eyes light up with even more anger and meanness in them.

Next, I said a stupid thing like "God just told me you are going to be our next kid." I asked him his name and where he came from. He didn't want to talk to me or anyone just then. He had just had another big fight with his parents. About that time, his mom came walking in, and he asked her, "Who in the hell is that lady?" She wasn't sure, but told him she thought I was Delaney Harmond, one of the youth leaders with Glenn and Bonnie Clark. He told her what I had said, gave me a dirty look and left.

The mother told me that the young man was her

adopted son, Jeff. Seventeen years ago, they had seen his picture as a tiny baby in a Christian magazine. They flew to Columbia, South America to adopt this five-month-old little boy. His parents were missionaries, but it seems they didn't realize the real mission they had taken on.

The parents later told me they had had nothing but problems with Jeff in the past few years. He spent most of his weekends and lots of time behind bars. The parents didn't know what else to do, but call the police and have him taken away.

I didn't understand all that, but I told the parents that I taught and worked behind bars with juvenile delinquent boys. I was sure my Bill and I could handle Jeff, and he'd stay out of trouble. I also told them if they couldn't handle the brat, just throw him and his suitcase on our door step. That very next weekend, there Jeff was with his suitcase on our door step. At the same time, we were heading out the door to help two darling, young missionary girls paint their new home on the water in Gig Harbor. Shale Ann and Tracy were pleased to see more help join us. Jeff was anything but pleased, but he did hang around and paint. We had a pizza party later that night, then all went home to bed really tired. Bill and I prayed for Jeff that he wouldn't run away (our boys did at times). Jeff stayed that night, and we loved him from the start.

He learned to love us later! He rededicated his life to the Lord, gave up selling and taking drugs, and no longer was stealing and lying. We put him in Gig Harbor High School, and he graduated. We were told it would never happen and that we could be wasting our time and money on Jeff. We knew a lot of damaged gang members and so-called bad kids never made it. But, God does not make junk and does love His creations.

Things went well for months, no house rules broken and no problems. Than after the "honeymoon" period was over, Jeff started testing us. He stayed out late, wasn't calling and checking in after school, etc. I jumped on his case and got in his face. I told him I loved him enough to not let him run wild. I also told him if he didn't like our rules then don't let our door hit him in the butt on his way out.

He left and slammed the door. Bill and I prayed for his safe return. We felt a real peace and this one, I didn't go looking for. Five days later, he called, tired of living in a garage with a friend. Of course, I drove and picked him up and brought him home. He stayed three years and became part of our family. He also made up with his adopted family and loves them dearly.

He started bringing other hurting kids to church, as well as home to us. Jeff even went to some of the homes he had robbed and asked for forgiveness, gave back and offered restitution.

One night, a group of us were feeding and giving clothing to the poor on the streets of Tacoma. I looked up and saw Jeff walking down the street in his stocking feet. I knew Jeff had on a new pair of white tennis shoes when we left home. I yelled at him, "Don't be walking in this dirty mess in socks only!" I then noticed a young man sitting, all dirty and worn, beside me, putting on Jeff's new shoes. I started crying as I realized what Jeff had done with his shoes.

Jeff laughed at me and said he was just doing what he knew I had done before. (The boys did watch us!)

That wasn't the first time I found him giving away his clothes, shoes or money and even bringing the homeless home. He helped lead several other gang members down the right path. I knew the day I saw this kid that he was special.

Jeff Herrmann, Regina, Josh

He met and brought to church a darling young girl. Brieanne and Jeff dated for two years and were married recently. Jeff wanted a church wedding, prayers and Jesus to be invited. His youth leader, Glenn Clark, performed this as his first wedding ceremony. What a precious ceremony it was! Jesus was truly there. He surrounded the church with a beautiful, double rainbow for the newlyweds to drive through as they left. We were all in awe.

It will be exciting to see the path these two have ahead of them. I'm sure it will be a blessed one.

Jeff and Brienne Herrmann

21
My Prayers Were Too Late

I've loved my 2 boys as much and maybe more than most mothers. I thank God for giving me this love and even extra love for other moms' kids. One of my favorite small ones is four-year-old Miles. I spend a lot of time with Miles. One day as I was hugging him he gave me more wise information (as he always does).

"I love you so much, Miles, and I so wish you were mine. You are a gift from God," I said.

Miles looked at me with his big blue eyes and smiled. He laughed as he said, "I love you, Delaney." Just then he jumped up from the couch and said. "Delaney! I just figured out why you didn't get me." He placed his little hands on his hips and with great concern he informed me of his answer. First of all

Miles, age 3 fell from a 90 foot cliff with only a few scratches

he told me that his mom, Katherin, has prayed for and asked God for him way before I did. Therefore, I was too slow, didn't pray fast enough as his mom had. God had heard his mom's prayers first and that's why I didn't get him.

So, now I can only be a sub-grandmom. And for that I am thankful.

Epilogue
Call of the Young, Wild Native

The rain was pouring down in a cold, wet stream that dark Friday night in Tacoma. It was November 1998 and I was downtown 15th Avenue with other Christians, feeding and giving out clothes to the street people. We'd been doing this for about four years. Others had been there giving for 15 years or more.

Ths one Friday night, I noticed a Native American mom and her nine children in line waiting to be fed and collecting clothing. My friend, Regina Holts, picked up the three-year-old and was playing with the nine-month-old baby and other small kids.

Suddenly, a flash of big saggy jeans, sloppy shirt and long ebony black hair flew past me. I reached out and grabbed hold of this flying object. It turned out to be a handsome, young 13-year-old, named Dobson, the fourth son of the Native American mom. The mother was friendly and talked with us about her family. All of this time, Dobson was running from me and teasing us. I yelled at him to settle down and that I felt God telling me to take this wild Indian of a kid home with me. (We had raised 43 other gang members and street kids. I knew here was *trouble*.) I told his mom I would like his phone number, unsure if he even had one. She said "great," try and get it from him. My friend Regina said "Don't worry. Delaney will get his number and the kid!"

At last, I got Dobson to look me in the face and talk to me. I asked if the "brat" would come to Gig Harbor with me for a weekend. He said 'hell, no!' and you can't have my number. I said that's okay. God will give it *and you* to me. He asked "What do you mean?" I said God had given me other boys to raise that were bigger, meaner, uglier and blacker than you are. Dobson laughed, sat down on the curb and scribbled a phone number on a scrap of paper. As he ran down the street again, I opened the slip of paper and read the phone number written in bold black lettering:

911

Little did we know I'd be using that number to rescue Dobson and his family...

Two worlds met on a Korean road

Order Form

To order additional copies of:

They call me a Rag Picker

Please send $10.95 plus $2.50 shipping/handling for each book. Washington residents please include 8.4% sales tax. Make check or money order payable to:

Designs by Delaney
4221 68th Street Ct. NW
Gig Harbor, WA 98335

253-851-7497
bharmond@prodigy.net

Name ————————————————————————
Address ————————————————————————
City, State, Zipcode ————————————————————

Copies ———— *@ $10.95 each* ——————
Shipping & Handling   ——————
WA state residents 8.4%   ——————
Total enclosed   ——————